101 *Deeper, Darker* Questions for Humanity

Coffee Table Philosophy

J Edward Neill

Cover Graphic by J Edward Neill

Tessera Guild Publishing

Téssera

ISBN-13: 978-1519577504
ISBN-10: 1519577508

To blow up any party anywhere.

Start asking questions to mess with people's minds...

...and stuff.

Special thanks to Jaylene and Melissa.

Welcome to the latest volume in the *Coffee Table Philosophy* series.

When I first settled in to write the *101 Questions* books, I didn't think I'd *ever* be able to create enough questions.

I figured humanity's dilemmas were finite and predictable. After all, how many different takes on life & death, good vs evil, and human interaction could there be? People are creatures of habit, I figured. We all do the same things over and over again.

Turns out I was wrong.

It's not about what people *do*.

It's what we *think* that's fascinating.

So here we are. 101 pages. 101 more questions.

I have to admit; research for this book was exceedingly fun. I scribbled questions on pieces of paper (a napkin, in one case) and wandered off to taverns, house parties, and even my buddy's *first date* with his new girlfriend. I asked guys, girls, and spent many a romantic evening pestering beautiful women with my questions.

Initially, people looked at me like I'd just fallen off the moon.

But after the first question sank in, the night belonged to me.

Because deep down, *everyone* has a dark side.

Six Deadly Sins

The 7 Deadly Sins are:

Envy

Greed

Sloth

Lust

Gluttony

Pride

Wrath

If you could destroy one of these *forever*, as in remove it from the consciousness of every human being for all time, which sin would you choose?

First Snowflake in the Avalanche

In your opinion, what is the *smallest* act by an enemy (against your home nation) that you would consider worthy of starting a full-scale war?

Anything by The Cure

Name at least one song you like that makes you sad whenever you listen to it.

And explain why you like it.

The Time Haters

Suppose someone truly evil comes to power during your lifetime.

This awful person enslaves thousands of people, steals billions of dollars, and kills whomever they want.

...whenever they want to.

Now suppose you have a time machine that can take you back exactly 100 years into the past.

Would you ever consider seeking out the evil person's ancestors and *removing them from the equation*?

If so, what would your method be?

The Unfriending

Which of the following *one-time occurrences* might cause you to lose your faith in a good friend?

- They fail to show up for a social event and never explain why
- You're forced to pay a large restaurant tab because they didn't bring any money
- While tipsy, they flirt with your significant other
- They borrow something and 'forget' to return it
- They send terrible gifts for birthdays and holidays
- They tell you 'white-lies' to spare your feelings

Forever Off the Grid

Suppose a person became extremely wealthy early in life.

By the time they're 30 years old, they've got billions of dollars in the bank.

Now suppose this person retires from any and all forms of work.

They don't have a job.

They don't do volunteer service.

They don't work for any charities.

They'll never have any children.

Is this person a bad human being?

Are they lazy? A total non-factor in society?

Or is it absolutely fine for someone to be this way?

The Chisel

You died yesterday.

Your family and friends commissioned a tombstone to forever mark your grave.

In terms of the life you've actually lived, what saying appears on your tombstone?

Suppose you'd lived ten years longer than yesterday. Given the extra time, what then would your tomb say?

And if an enemy or rival of yours were to engrave your tomb, what would they write?

Life Long or Die Hard

In Shakespeare's play, *Julius Caesar*, the following line is uttered:

"Cowards die many times before their deaths;
The valiant never taste of death but once."

In other words, Shakespeare means to say that those who live in fear die a small death every time they back away from something that terrifies them.

Do you agree with this?

Why or why not?

Rank and File

In your opinion, is any one branch of the military *braver* than the others?

For example, are Marines braver than fighter pilots?

Do infantry soldiers have more courage than the crew of a submarine?

Honesty Setting: 90%

Among most humans, it's assumed not everyone is completely
honest 100% of the time.

Some people exaggerate.

Other people understate.

Others leave out details so as not to offend whoever's listening.

If you could choose an honesty setting for all the people in your
life, what % would you pick?

And what's your personal honesty setting?

A Day of Infamy

Suppose everyone alive knew the exact date of their death.
Not the method or cause, *just the date.*

If your death were scheduled to be twenty years from now, would
you live any differently than you currently do?

What if your death were only *five* years away?

If for either situation you said you'd change your way of life,
shouldn't you change it now anyway? ☺

Gandalf the *Black*?

Suppose magic is real and every person can learn one specific power to claim as their own.

What power will you wield?

What will your 'wizard' name be?

Is there any one part of your day that is absolutely sacred to you?
As in a small daily moment, a place in time, an everyday activity,
or a meal?

Also…

Is there any part of your daily life you dread? As in; you'd live
happier without it?

Behind the Veil

Throughout history, many millions of people have reported seeing ghosts, apparitions, aliens, monsters, and other strange, unexplainable phenomena.

Which of the following do *you* believe probably exist?

Ghosts

Aliens

Angels

Demons

ESP (extra-sensory perception)

Alternate Dimensions

Got any proof? ☺

If there is such a thing...

In ten words or fewer, state your personal definition of LOVE.

Heart of Darkness

And now, in ten words or fewer, state your personal definition of HATE.

Silver Tongues

What is the worst lie you've ever told?

If you're reluctant to answer, then…

…what is the worst lie someone has ever told you?

And why?

Peak and Valley

For you personally, what is the absolute best part about sex?

And...

What's the hardest part about sleeping with a new person?

(no pun intended)

Mic Drop

Other than winning the lottery, name three things that would make you want to immediately walk away from your job.

As in; tomorrow morning you pack up your things and never go back.

Hard Scales of Justice

Imagine the following scenarios.

In which of these (if any) would you support the *death penalty*?

- After fifty years of marriage, an elderly woman shoots her husband in his sleep. Her motivation is to claim life insurance money
- A pair of eleven-year old boys lure a little girl into the woods, where they murder her for no apparent reason
- A man foreign to your native country guns down ten people in a small, peaceful café
- A politician orders your military to bomb a village in another country, killing *one* enemy combatant and *two-hundred* civilians

Calculus

Fill in the blanks. No more than two words each.

_____

$+$

_____

$=$

the best reasons for living.

Automatica

Do you think humanity will ever reach a point of not having to work?

As in; *everything* will be automated.

Labor won't be needed.

Everyone will have unlimited leisure time.

Is this something humanity should try to achieve?

Is it a future you'd embrace?

Dying Stars and Sabertooth Tigers

Name something that is both *beautiful* AND *terrifying* to you.

Venus & Mars

This is an exercise for couples.

…or even platonic friends, so long as one is a guy and the other is a girl.

Give each guy and girl a pen and one sheet of paper.

With a 60-second time limit, everyone writes down their personal answer to:

What five things are needed to make a perfect date?

And then everyone shares.

How different are the answers between the sexes?

Little Bang Theory

Some people have theories about how the world began.

And how it will end.

And maybe even theories about what it all means.

But...

What if you— *yes you*—could decide how it all began, what it all

means, and how you'd like it to end?

Play god for a moment:

How would *you* like for the universe to have begun?

How do *you* want it to end?

What do *you* want it all to mean?

The Last Bottle's Bottom

It's entirely possible humanity will never develop the ability to
leave Earth and spread out to live among the stars.

If so, how do you imagine the *very last human* will die?

Picket Fences

You're *madly* in love.

Tomorrow you'll have the chance to marry the love of your life.

You'll have a huge house full of beautiful things.

Your children will be smart and loving.

On the surface, your marriage will appear ideal.

But here's the thing: You've glimpsed the future and have seen that while your marriage will be stable and polite, it will ultimately become passionless and empty.

Knowing what you know, are you still walking down the aisle tomorrow?

Angel of Death

You *lucky* bastard.

Or maybe not.

You've just acquired a new ability.

From now on, you can wish anyone in the world dead.

If you use this power, not only will the person die instantly and painlessly, but you'll also gain a million dollars for each person you use it on.

How many times (if any) do you think you'll use this power?

On whom?

What would you do with all that money?

Idealistic

For the following situations, state whether you believe each one is *society's* job or the job of the individual *family*:

- Extending the life of a terminally ill patient
- Doing the same ↑ for someone who is a war veteran
- Providing treatment for a criminally insane person
- Providing a free college education
- Providing welfare for underprivileged children
- Caring for the elderly

Little Pharma

Turns out you're in the pharmaceutical industry.

And you've just invented the pill of a lifetime.

Used once daily, whoever takes it becomes immune to

_____.

_____ can be whatever you want it to be, but it can only

be *one* thing.

A disease. A mental condition. A state of mind. Whatever.

Fill in _____.

Can we Talk?

Take a brief trip into your own past.

What's one piece of advice you'd give your younger self?

Extinction Level Events

Choose one animal species on Earth to utterly eliminate. Consider all the repercussions of their absence.

Now choose an extinct species to revive and return to a healthy population level.

Explain both your choices.

Protect this House

Name two instances in which it's ok to be completely selfish.

The Heist

If you could steal any *one* thing in the world and make it yours

forever, what would it be?

It can be an object, a person, a life situation, a place.

You won't get in any trouble for taking it.

No one will ever know.

Well?

Monopoly Money

You've just received three GET-OUT-OF-*DEATH*-FREE cards.

Anyone who has one of these avoids the next time they would die.

Once a death is avoided, the card vanishes.

So…

Keeping all three for yourself?

Giving any away?

Distribute your cards and explain.

Fix-it Felix

What is humanity's biggest flaw?

i.e.; What's the one weakness we all possess that you'd like to put
an end to.

Got any suggestions for fixing it?

Soul Mining

Imagine you have no work to do.

You have a free home and vehicle.

All your food is prepared for you at no cost.

100% of your time is reserved for leisure.

Even if you wanted to get a job, you couldn't. There are *none*.

The catch: you have no money for expensive vacations, travel, or

lavish entertainment.

What will you do with all your free time?

9 Billion Vampires

Suppose 100 years from now humanity perfects a sustainable
scientific method for extending human life.

Indefinitely.

Meaning everyone everywhere receives an annual treatment that
effectively makes them immortal. No diseases. No aging. No
natural death.

What are some of the problems you foresee should this ever
happen?

Design two laws you think would be needed to maintain peace and
prosperity among an immortal population.

Circuits Crossed

Can feminism and chivalry co-exist?

As in; pure, genuine chivalry and sharp, dedicated-to-equality feminism?

Explain.

Nectar of the Gods

Suppose you had a single bottle of the most delicious drink ever to exist.

It's the perfect beverage, smooth as silk, subtle and intoxicating, and utterly refreshing.

There's only one bottle of this nectar left in the world.

So...

What occasion would you use to drink it?

Would you finish it off in one night or spread it out over a longer period?

Would you share it with anyone?

The Vow

Suppose right here and now you are compelled to make an *oath*. Meaning you'll kneel on the ground, say some sacred stuff, and commit to fulfilling this oath for as long as you shall live.

It can be anything you want, but it must require a lifetime of obligation.

What is your life-oath?

Metaphysical Exam

Of the following qualities, pick the two you'd most want as traits
of a close friend.

Brutally honest

Entirely non-judgmental

Rarely complains

Never envious or jealous

Extremely creative

Always the fun one

Highly responsible

Now choose again (just two) to be traits of your lover or spouse.

Any difference?

On a Scale of 0-10…

…in which 0 is 'not at all', 5 is average, and 10 means '*highly*':

How intelligent are you?

How physically attractive are you?

How charming?

How artistic?

How generous?

And how narcissistic?

Needs of the Many

Imagine you and *ninety-nine* other people are fleeing through the
wilderness.

A vicious, unstoppable beast pursues you, but for the moment has
lost your trail.

The only problem: an infant child in your group has begun to wail,
howl, and cry uncontrollably. If it continues, the beast will surely
hear the noise and devour all one-hundred of you.

So...

The baby isn't going to stop crying anytime soon.

What do you do?

Population *Destiny*

At the time this book was written, the approximate population of
Earth is 7,200,000,000.

That's 7.2 billion human beings.

Now suppose tomorrow you wake up and Earth's population is
only 10% of this.

As in only 720,000,000 – distributed evenly across the globe.

Would everyone's life be *better*?

Worse?

What do you think it'd be like to live on Earth with a population
density so low compared to now?

Mirror, Mirror, on the Wall

In your own words, define what you believe the difference is between a terrorist and a normal soldier.

Swords and Cajones

Imagine everything in the world is exactly as it is right now.

Except...

No modern weapons exist. No guns, missiles, bombs, warplanes, tanks, nukes, etc.

Instead, war is fought with swords, spears, axes, and shields.

It's *medieval*.

Would there still be just as much warfare?

Getting Around

From the following scenarios, choose the most appealing to you:

- Be happily married to one person for your entire life. Never once have an affair
- Be happily married for twenty happy years, but also enjoy a twenty-year period of single-dom, during which you have sex with at least ten different partners
- Never be married. Have as much freedom and as many different sex partners as you desire
- Insert a different answer here _____

Shopping Lists for Gods

You've just woken up and found one billion dollars in your account.

The money is legit. It's all yours.

Using percentage values between 1-100%, define what percent of your money you'd use for:

Savings

Entertainment

Housing

Vehicles/Transportation

Charity

Gifts to family

Your %'s must total 100.

Daggers for the Sky

You've been assigned a monumental task.

Literally.

Over the next twenty years, you'll be the project leader for ten-thousand workers as they construct a monument to represent all of humanity.

You have a one-billion dollar budget.

You have total creative control.

What do you instruct your workers to create?

Ctrl, Alt, *Delete*

What's one email, text, or phone call you wish you could go back and *undo*?

180 Degrees

Suppose a man dedicated the first twenty years of his life to being
a vicious criminal.

He was a thief, a thug, an arsonist, a kidnapper, and even a
murderer.

But then, for the next 50 years, he turned his life around.

He gave millions to charity. He found homes for orphans. He fed
the poor. He traveled to war-torn nations and helped innocent
people evacuate.

What is the value of this man's life?

In your eyes, has he found redemption?

Hot for Teacher

You're going to be a teacher for one month.

Your class: *every five-year old child in the entire world.*

Given the chance, what lesson would you teach these kids?

What if they were all fifteen-year olds?

Scientists have created a new and powerful type of remote control.
With it, you can choose something in the world to turn on or off.
—At any time. From any place. No matter the distance.—
How it works:
You pre-program the remote to turn on or off one *specific* machine,
electronic device, vehicle, emotion, or even a person.
This pre-programming works only on one thing. Ever.

What's your remote *control*?

_____ **wanted**

You've just started a new company.

You make, market, and sell stuff all around the world.

Which of the following people are you most likely to hire?

- *A beautiful woman fresh out of college*
- *A sharply intelligent, but socially awkward young man*
- *An older veteran skilled in the ins and outs of business*
- *A tireless, hard-working middle-aged man without a degree*
- *A middle-aged woman who excels at team-building*

Explain your choice.

Unshakeable

Consider your core beliefs.

Concentrate on the ones regarding the Earth, your fellow humans, and your spirituality.

Is there one belief among these that you don't think you could ever be swayed on?

If so, explain why.

Generations of Evil

In certain cultures around the world, different generations are referred to *separately*.

For example, in America there exist such divisions as Gen-X, Baby Boomers, and The Greatest Generation.

It's a common theme for older generations to criticize those who are younger, often with cries of, "Kids these days don't know a damn thing!"

Is it true that previous generations contain people who are wiser, harder working, and more moral?

Or has every generation that has ever existed contained similar percentages of stupid, lazy, and immoral people?

Part-Timer

The word 'hero' is used a lot nowadays.

So...

Are some people truly heroes? As in always?

Or do some people sometimes do heroic things…
…after which they get labeled as a hero for life?

Taxation with Representation

Suppose you were able to choose *exactly* what your tax dollars funded.

In this new system, a survey will arrive in the mail each year.

You'll get to check boxes based on what projects you want your money to be used for.

Name two things you'd definitely want your taxes to fund.

And two things you'd never, ever use taxes to pay for.

Bank of Humanity

Do we as human beings have any responsibility to:

Help the homeless?

Put our lives at risk to save fellow humans in danger?

Raise our children to respect cultural norms?

Honor the traditions of the nation in which we live?

Look out for our neighbors?

Revenge Algebra

Complete the following equation.
Use no more than three words per blank.

_____

$+$

_____

$=$

A suitable punishment for a serial killer

Professionals

For each of the following, state whether or not you believe it's a low-class or shameful profession:

Garbage Removal

Pizza Delivery

Prostitution

Exotic Dancing

Professional Gambling

Weapons Manufacturer

Slum Landlord

Politician

While They're Standing on a Cliff's Edge

Tomorrow you're going to find out that your spouse, fiancée, or lover has been cheating on you (vigorously) for many months.

If you had to choose, *how* would you want to learn about it?

Stumble across some emails?

Overhear a phone conversation?

Walk in on them while they're _____ing?

Some other way?

Shoot for the Moon

Consider *everyone* else in the room with you.

For each person, imagine a gift you'd like to give them.

This gift can be anything: physical, emotional, spiritual, etc.

You can only give them one thing.

Your imagination is the only limit.

SPF 1,000,000

You deserve a break after answering piles of deep philosophical questions.

So...

If after your death you could live on as a vampire, would you? You'd have to sip human blood and avoid the sun at all costs. But otherwise you'd be pretty much immortal.

AK-Forty Whatever

Imagine you can build a special kind of gun.

This gun has *unlimited* ammunition. You can load it with anything imaginable. You only get one choice.

Bullets. Lasers. Rockets.

Money. Medicine. Liquor.

Sweet dreams. Happiness. Orgasms.

Or something else.

What's in your gun?

Super Mega Awesome Eve

Invent a new national holiday.

No businesses will be open on this day.

Everyone will celebrate it.

What day of the year is your new holiday?

What's the day called?

Destitution

Finish the following sentences:

The *poorest* person alive is he who _____.

The *richest* person is she who _____.

Nutshells

Use one word in each blank:

_____

$+$

_____

$=$

The meaning of your life.

Love Fades

Consider your life's passion.

It's your goal, your end-game, the fire beneath your bottom.

Now…

Name something that could make you give this passion up.

Cyborgs

Imagine that technology exists to improve the human body via cybernetic upgrades.

In other words, for the right price, you can replace any portion of your body with a powerful and aesthetically pleasing robotic version.

Arms. Legs. Eyes. Organs. Et cetera.

Assume a 300% improvement for each upgrade.

Will you do it?

If so, which two body parts will you upgrade first?

You are Legend

Imagine the apocalypse has struck.

Every single human in the world has died.

Except you.

Aside from survive, what will you do during the long, empty years

ahead of you?

Be specific.

Job Security

Suppose you could ingest a government-issued drug that would
extend your life to approximately 200 years.
You'll age only 25% as quickly if you take this drug.

The catch:

You'll have to work at the same job for the entirety of your life.
Would you take the drug?
What specific job or trade would you commit to mastering?

The Lifeboat

The old saying goes, "Women and children first."

Meaning: if there's grave danger at hand, women and children

should be rescued first.

The men be damned.

Do you agree with this premise?

The Island

In this exercise, you will build your perfect *sanctuary*.

You have only the following rules:
This place will be utterly removed from the rest of the universe
You will be the only inhabitant
It will be exactly one square mile in size
You can fill it with any landscapes, buildings, climate, and animals
you desire, but no people
You will exist alone there for one-thousand years

Now build.

Worms in the Same Apple

Which of the following three people is the most vile?

Someone who manipulates *others* to do terrible things (Hitler, Stalin, Pol Pot.)

Someone who *willingly* does terrible things under the command or desire of another (Nazis, etc.)

Someone indifferent who stands by and does *nothing* while the innocent suffer?

Paranoia

Imagine someone in real life wants to kill you.

Who among your family, friends, frienemies, and associates is this person most likely to be?

What's the most likely reason they'd want *you* gone?

Stereotypes

Do you believe a person's personality can be predicted based on any of the following?

The music they listen to?

Their job?

The television shows they watch?

Their marital status?

Their looks?

The Artisan

Tomorrow you'll wake up with a new skill of your choice.

You'll be the best in the world at this one thing.

You can pick only one skill.

Choose this new talent carefully.

A Dark Day

For one single 24-hour day, you get to be an all-powerful *villain*.

During this day, the world is yours to rule.

You can act with total impunity.

You can satisfy any desire, no matter how depraved.

You can commit heinous crimes without being punished.

At the day's end, the world resets to normal and all the evil you

may or may not have done vanishes from existence.

Describe your day in detail.

Think you'd enjoy it?

The Hunger

Every human being is born with the desire and the need to eat,

drink, reproduce, and survive.

This instinct includes the will to compete for resources, to fight,

and even to *destroy* if threatened.

Most of these instincts don't have to be taught.

They just are.

Knowing that, is there truly such a thing as *innocence*?

Woulda Shoulda Coulda

Should:

...politicians be allowed to receive money from special-interest groups?

...women be allowed to serve in military infantry divisions?

...most drugs be legalized?

...companies be allowed to fire employees for whatever reason they want?

...standardized testing be eliminated?

...fortune cookies be required to contain actual fortunes, not just random statements?

Have you ever suddenly and completely reversed your personal position regarding a major component of your life?

Such as: your religious beliefs, your political tendencies, or the way you felt about an important cultural/social event.

If so, explain in detail.
If not, why so hard-headed? ☺

Wash the Chalkboard

You've had a terrible accident.

All of your memories have been completely wiped out.

Except one.

Choose the one single memory you'd want to keep above all others.

The Slayer

Once.

That's all you get to use this next power.

Just one time, you get to slay anything in the world.

One person.

One thing.

One idea.

One way of life.

Anything you want: Dead

So, killer…

What'll it be?

Tick or Tock

For each of the following proverbs or ideals, call out *yes* or *no*. Yes means you support it. No means you reject it or you're not so sure:

An eye for an eye

A picture is worth a thousand words

Expectation is the root of all heartache

History is written by men who have hanged heroes

Whatever we think, we become

After the game, kings and pawns go in the same box

Keep your friends close. Keep your enemies closer

Explain your answer to at least one of these.

Talk is Cheap

On a scale of $1.00 to $100.00, what value does an opinion have if it's stated by someone who *thinks* about the issue at hand, but *does* nothing?

Now estimate how many $1.00 opinions you've had in your life.

Seriously.

Permanent Vacation

You're taking a trip.

A *looooooooooooong* trip.

It'll last for thirty years, during which you and *one* other person

will travel together to and from an interstellar paradise.

No one else is coming with you.

So…

Who's your travel mate?

And why them?

Jesus F#^(ing Christ

Name a cause you'd be willing to become a martyr for.

As in *you die*, and the cause succeeds because of it.

A Price for Everything

If you could guarantee yourself a peaceful, healthy life (*not necessarily happy,* but peaceful and healthy) which of the following, *if any*, would you be willing to give up?

Sex

Alcohol

Your pets

Music

Good food

Family

Love

Open Heart Surgery

Tell everyone in the room about the *love of your life*.

It doesn't necessarily have to be a romantic love.

It can be a person, an animal, a passion…

If no one else is in the room with you, skip this question until a later time.

But if other people are here, open your heart for all to see.

Just be careful not to surprise your wife. ☺

The Exhumer

You've been given a one-time power.

With it, you can resurrect any one thing, as in bring it back to life.

It can be a person.

An animal.

An object.

An idea.

A tradition.

A cultural norm.

What will you resurrect?

Change your Underwear

Name at least one thing that makes you weak in the knees.

Explain why.

War Against Heaven

In John Milton's epic poem, Paradise Lost, the angel Lucifer rebels against his creator.

His motivations are jealousy (for his creator's love of mankind) as well as a desire to no longer spend *eternity* at his master's feet.

Given the situation, if *you* were in Lucifer's shoes (or hooves ☺) would you rebel?

Would you be jealous of your creator's love for an inferior species?

Would you wage war to be free of a master you believed didn't value you?

Rock, Paper, Machine Gun

Which one of the following three human traits is most powerful?

Intelligence (Our minds)

Emotions (Our passions)

Instincts (Our biology)

Answer for humanity at large and for yourself.

Bottom of the World

Imagine…

Your whole life, you've been looking for something.

You've traveled far and wide. You've climbed mountains. You've plumbed the depths of the deepest ocean trench.

Finally one day you learn the object of your desire rests in the lowest chamber of the world's deepest cavern.

You go there. You find a treasure chest. You unlock it.

What's inside the chest?

What's the one thing you've searched your whole life for, but you've never been able to find?

Told You So

If you had to guess, which of the following events is most likely to cause the end of the human race?

A meteor strikes Earth

A terrible disease infects everyone

Nuclear warfare

We invent artificial intelligence, which in turn destroys us

The Sun goes supernova

A higher being wipes us out

Aliens

Or _____

Sensory Deprivation

What would you miss most if tomorrow you:

Went suddenly blind

Lost your sense of smell

Went deaf

Lost your ability to taste

Lost all sensation of touch

?

Assume each condition is permanent.

Be specific about what you'd miss.

Democrachy

Suppose you are the ruler of a new nation.

In general terms, what kind of government will you institute?

(Create a new government type if you want.)

One _____ to Rule them All

Is it morally wrong to desire power?

The Definition of Darkness

It's a fair assumption that almost all people have had dark thoughts
from time to time.

Racist thoughts.

Misogynistic thoughts.

Dark sexual fantasies.

Perhaps even visions of destruction, murder, and violence.

So…

What's your personal darkness?

What's something you've thought of, accidentally or otherwise,
that might terrify the people who know you?

If you enjoyed reading 101 Deeper, Darker Questions for

Humanity, please consider leaving an Amazon review.

☺

A thousand years from today, nearly all of humanity is jacked-In.

We sleep, connected to machines, dreaming our lives away.

Read J Edward Neill's

J Edward's Books:

Coffee Table Philosophy:
The Ultimate Get to Know Someone Quiz

Reality is Best Served with Red Wine

Life & Dark Liquor

The Small Book of BIG Questions

444 Questions for the Universe

Big Shiny Red Buttons

101 Questions for Single People

101 Questions for Couples

101 Reasons to Break Up

Fiction:
A Door Never Dreamed Of

Hollow Empire – Night of Knives

The Hecatomb

Eaters of the Light series:
Darkness Between the Stars

Shadow of Forever

Eater of the Light

Tyrants of the Dead trilogy:
Down the Dark Path

Dark Moon Daughter

Nether Kingdom

About the Author

J Edward Neill writes philosophy and fiction for adult audiences. He resides in North Georgia, where the summers are volcanic and winters don't exist. He has an extensive sword collection, a deep love of wine and scotch, and a chubby grey cat named Noodle.

He's really just a ghost.

He's here to haunt the earth for few more decades.

Shamble after J Edward on his websites:

TesseraGuild.com

DownTheDarkPath.com

□Téssera

Made in the USA
San Bernardino, CA
12 June 2019